A Nostalgic Journey...

...Back to the Sixties

BRITISH LORRIES

OF THE SIXTIES

First published in 1991 by Roundoak Publishing
(an imprint of Nynehead Books), Nynehead,
Wellington, Somerset TA21 0BX, England.

British Library Cataloguing In Publication Data

Davies, Peter
        1.Trucks-Great Britain-History
        I.Title
        629.2'24

ISBN 1-871565-09-X

Designed by Peter Davies

Jacket photograph: Dating from 1960 this
Gardner-engined Atkinson L946 drawbar outfit
from the well-known Suttons of St Helens fleet
bridges the transition from the old era to the
new. It first went to work in a world of 24-ton
gvw eight wheelers but within only five years
new 32-ton artics were taking over the lead role
in UK haulage.

This book is dedicated to my father, Evan
Edward Davies, who died in December 1990 at
the age of 79. He spent much of his working life
as a driver, his main employers being Crosville
Motor Services and the Milk Marketing Board.

Composition by Ryburn Typesetting Ltd,
Luddendenfoot, Halifax, West Yorkshire.

Printed in Great Britain by The Amadeus Press
Ltd, Huddersfield, West Yorkshire.

Contents

Bathed in the weak morning sun, this scene along Bury Old Road, Manchester, depicts a 1967 Foden S21 'Mickey Mouse' eight wheeled tipper from Mullan Bros of Chesterfield.

One look at this picture is worth a thousand words. It captures the very essence of British haulage. A 1961 AEC 'Mk.V' Mammoth Major heads towards its base in Kent loaded high and sheeted in the correct fashion with two dollies to each rope. This perfectly balanced machine exhibits all the best characteristics of a working lorry at its peak. The front discharge exhaust bellows out a healthy roar. 'Well sat down' on the rear springs, sans spare wheel, front tyre blackened by exhaust smoke – it has it all.

The driver casts an anxious glance at the camera, possibly concerned that he is being spied on by a Ministry man. Far from wishing to spoil such a spectacle with thoughts of Ministry men, the photographer (and author of this book) was quietly savouring the scene, knowing that such vehicles would soon be disappearing from the roads. By 1969 most of them had. Happily the AEC depicted here survived as a recovery vehicle and during 1990–91 was restored back to original condition by its owners, Alan Firmin Ltd.

PREFACE

This book does not set out simply to catalogue all the various British makes model by model. Instead it records Britain's best known lorries exactly as they appeared at work. Because of the wide variety of bodywork and liveries every vehicle has its own individual character. While most transport books feature photographs of lorries in new condition, some even before registration and painting, this volume concentrates on lorries as they appeared in operation. Whether work-worn and heavily laden, or gleaming with fresh paint, they appear exactly as they were seen at work. That is the only way they should be remembered. Think of this as a unique opportunity to recapture lost memories of a past era.

How often have we longed to go back in time to relive enjoyable experiences? Imagine being granted an opportunity to revisit the Sixties – to stand and watch the lorries on the A5, the A1 or along the newly opened M1 motorway. It was a very different scene from today's – AEC Mk.Vs, Power Plus Leylands with the LAD Vista-View cabs and Mickey Mouse Fodens could be seen in abundance. Such vehicles are now extinct save for a handful surviving in preservation.

Often the only existing records of lorries are in the form of manufacturers' black and white press photographs which usually lack working atmosphere. Operators' liveries are so important that much of the material in this book has been reproduced in colour, bringing alive once more the full character of the lorries as they really appeared twenty to thirty years ago. In many cases these are the only existing colour records.

All the photographs reproduced in this book are by the author. Most of them have been shot on a simple camera and if they lack technical quality it is due in part to the fact that all camera settings had to be guessed. I had no form of light meter, range finder or tripod. All shots were hand held and shutter speeds, apertures and focus settings based on pure guesswork. Colour shots are on transparency film which allowed little margin for error. It is therefore no surprise that some might be darker or lighter than they should be. However imperfect the pictures, they all serve to recall some precious instant in time and together I hope they will take you on a nostalgic journey through a transport scene which has quietly faded into history – that of Britain in the Sixties.

Peter Davies, August 1991

ERA OF CHANGE

The title of a popular song released in the mid Sixties,"The Times They Are A Changin'", could aptly sum up the transport scene in Britain during those years. At the very beginning of the decade haulage operators were adjusting to the new motorway age, the first stretch of the M1 having been opened in November 1959. It soon became clear that the vehicles which had served their purposes well in the Forties and Fifties were less than a match for the faster journey times made possible by motorways. Coupled with this there was a growing need to handle longer, heavier ISO shipping containers.

It was time for the old order to give way to the new. Maximum trailer lengths had been limited to about 26ft (7.9m) under the old legislation which, with only minor amendments, had been in force since the early Thirties. Legal payloads had been limited to about 16 tons. To harmonise with European standards UK operators needed to cope with 20-ton payloads in 40ft (l2m) containers. This called for higher axle weights, higher gross weights and increased length limits.

It all came about with the new 1964 Construction & Use Regulations. For the first time in the UK 32-ton gcw artics became legal and the impact of this soon changed the face of Britain's transport scene. Lingering remnants of the old 24-ton gross rigid eight era lived on throughout the Sixties, but most leading hauliers switched to artics. The 1964 regulations only allowed an extra 7ft (2.4m) overall length for artics which still did not permit the use of 40ft (12m) trailers. Hauliers had to wait until 1968 for the length to be raised to 15m and even then not all tractor/trailer combinations could easily stay within this limit. The artic boom had other effects – numerous rigids were cut down into tractor units and large numbers of imported tractors began to appear. While trailer manufacturers enjoyed a bonanza, British truck builders worked hard to meet the demand for high-powered, purpose-built 32-ton artics. However, most European manufacturers had existing models in their ranges to meet the new regulations. By the mid Sixties Britain's cosy world of AECs and ERFs was being infiltrated by 'strangers'. Such unfamiliar names as Mercedes Benz, Volvo, Scania-Vabis, Magirus-Deutz and DAF began to appear.

Heavier weights and higher speeds also focused attention on safety. More legislation emerged in the late Sixties aimed at tightening up on vehicle maintenance and driving standards. From 1968 annual HGV testing was phased in and the minimum standards, especially with regard to braking performance, sounded the death knell for many of the older lorries even if they had survived the artic onslaught. By the end of the Sixties the British haulage scene had changed quite considerably.

UK manufacturers were less dominant in their own market place. The traditional engine and gearbox manufacturers like Gardner and David Brown were also having to face competition from such manufacturers as Cummins and Fuller.

At the lower end of the weight range the impact of Sixties legislation was, perhaps, less noticeable. Exemption from HGV driver's licencing for lorries under 7.5 tons gross weight led to some increase in that category, while the introduction of 16-ton gross four wheelers made possible in 1964 diminished the numbers of twin steer 'Chinese Six' rigids. The use of drawbar trailers behind eight wheelers became less common while there was, if anything, an increase in four wheeler and trailer combinations. This was aided by the rescission of the 'second man' rule under which a statutory attendant had to accompany the driver on all journeys.

Along with the decline in traditional British lorries came the virtual end of coachbuilt cabs. Among the last lorries to feature them were the AEC Mk.V, the Foden S20, the ERF KV and the Atkinson range. In their place came welded pressed steel cabs like the Leyland Group 'Ergomatic' and fibreglass examples from Foden, Scammell and ERF. The period saw widening use of 'off-the-peg' steel cabs from Motor Panels which were fitted by Guy, Seddon, Scammell, Foden and ERF.

Atkinson was probably the very last to offer a traditional style cab in the form of the Mk.2 which appeared in 1968. Attempts to market more modern designs in the form of the Guardsman in 1964 and the Viewline in 1966 were less than successful. But it seemed that British operators had a soft spot for the dignified, old fashioned lines of the Mk.2 and it survived until the introduction of the new tilt cab Seddon Atkinson 400 Series in 1975.

There was a noticeable reduction in the number of individual manufacturers. It was an era when the Leyland Group expanded to absorb several other companies on the basis that a big group could compete more effectively in the world market. Already with Albion and Scammell under their wing, from 1951 and 1955 respectively, Leyland proceeded to take over the ACV Group, which consisted of AEC and Thornycroft, in 1962. The names Maudslay and Crossley had already disappeared within ACV. Light commercial manufacturers Standard were absorbed in 1961 and Bristol Commercial Vehicles in 1965. By this time Bristol had ceased production of their heavy goods models.

In 1968 British Motor Holdings which included Austin, Morris and Guy merged with Leyland to form the British Leyland Motor Corporation. This meant that one-time independents AEC, Albion, Austin, BMC, Guy, Leyland, Morris, Scammell and Thornycroft now all belonged to one group.

One inevitable outcome of big amalgamation is rationalisation, not only in production facilities but also in product lines. After all, within the vast range of truck models produced by those ten companies, there was a great deal of duplication especially in the four wheelers.

For instance, AEC's Mercury competed with Albion's Super Clydesdale, Leyland's Super Comet, Guy's Big J4 and eventually with the Boxers and Mastiffs of the Redline range. Similar duplication existed in the vast range of tractor units and, to an extent, in the six wheel and eight wheel rigids. The process of rationalisation was gradual but it was taking place throughout the late Sixties. Cross-pollination of group engines, gearboxes and axles meant that individual identities were becoming blurred.

Simplification of the model range accelerated in the Seventies, culminating with the disappearance of some models and eventually some makes.

Within the BLMC empire the once-proud names of AEC, Albion, Guy, Scammell and even Leyland itself lost some of their self respect when their famous name badges were replaced by the somewhat anonymous corporate badge featuring an 'L' in a 'catherine wheel'. The full effect of this process did not unfold until the Seventies, most of the marques having clung on to the remnants of their individuality through to the end of the Sixties.

Another development which began during the Sixties was the narrowing of the distinction between mass-produced trucks and, to use current terminology, 'premium' trucks. The lower cost mass produced trucks whose parentage lay in the car giants, like Austin, Vauxhall, Ford and Morris, represented one camp. Dodge and Commer products too tended to be linked more with that end of the market. AEC, Albion, Atkinson, ERF, Foden, Guy, Leyland and Scammell were, on the other hand, regarded as higher cost quality machines. Seddon and Dennis were linked more to this upper end. Between the two camps there was a clear gap both in price and quality. Although there was some overlap in weight ratings, the cheaper models concentrated on four wheelers and tractors up to about 12 tons payload, whereas the 'premium' vehicles ranged from about 6/7 tons payload up to maximum weight eight wheelers and artics.

It was in the Sixties that the gulf between the two camps began to close. This was particularly noticeable when Ford and Bedford began to move up the weight scale. These traditionally low cost makes moved into the heavy market in 1966 to produce 16-ton gvw four wheelers and 24-ton gcw tractors. At that time their pricing was still competitive compared with the true 'heavies' but during the next decade the price gap narrowed too. In the latter half of the Sixties several European makes, including Volvo, Mercedes, DAF, Fiat and Scania-Vabis appeared on the market.

Manufacturers who had their origins solely in heavy commercial vehicles, like AEC, Atkinson, ERF, Foden and Leyland, began to lose ground to these and their lower cost domestic competition in the late Sixties. The 'heroic' style of engineering associated with steam wagons was on the way out. Such manufacturers had to adapt to a more modern approach or go under. 'Off-the-peg' steel cabs and a wider choice of mechanical units from Eaton, Fuller, Cummins and Perkins were better tuned to the high speed age. They also saved the high cost of in-house design and development. Out went the old fasioned worm drive axles and Gardners lost their almost exclusive hold on sections of the heavy market.

Amidst these changes some heavy manufacturers still found the time and resources to explore futuristic projects by which the Sixties will be remembered. One was the streamlined BP Autotanker which formed a special attraction at the 1960 Commercial Motor Show. The main development for this was the responsibility of tank manufacturers Thompson Bros of Bilston, Staffs and Leyland supplied the

running units. This highly innovative 4000-gal tanker eventually went into service in Denmark. At the time it was probably seen as a blueprint for the tanker of the future but only the one was ever built.

Innovative features of the Autotanker included a transverse rear-mounted Leyland O.680 engine and four-speed Pneumo-Cyclic gearbox. Front suspension combined steel-leaf with air. Fully integral construction from aluminium alloy produced a sleek, ultra futuristic exterior and the laden centre of gravity was well below that of a conventional tanker. One highly questionable feature was its small cab entrance hatch in the front panel where the radiator would normally be. How the poor driver would have escaped in an emergency was anyone's guess. At least when seated in the cab he had the novelty of a nautical style periscopic rear view system.

The same year Scammell came up with their tanker of the future, the Trunker I. A five-axle 30-ton gcw outfit, it featured a version of the LAD cab faired into a fully panelled shell which concealed the chassis and its Gardner 6HLX 150 bhp horizontal underfloor engine. Single tyres were fitted all round. The Trunker I could boast a slightly better market penetration – three were built, registered 377, 378 and 379BGO, all seeing service with Shell BP.

Scammell Trunker I

Perhaps the most adventurous project in the Sixties came from Leylands in the form of their experimental gas turbine. The ultimate product of their development appeared in 1968. The Rover Car Co, who became part of the Leyland Group in 1966, had been active in the field gas turbine vehicles as early as 1952. After the acquisition of Rover, Leyland Gas Turbines Ltd was set up to concentrate on the development of a heavy truck. It was to be a three-axle tractor with a version of the Ergomatic cab and designed for 38-ton gcw operation at sustained speeds of around 70 mph.

The 350/400 bhp gas turbine engine revved at 30000 rpm geared down to 3000. It was half the weight of a comparable diesel and reckoned to incur only half the maintenance costs. Fuel consumption was claimed to be comparable with that of a diesel. To achieve the braking effect of a diesel on overrun, the variable power turbine nozzles swung into reverse. Four prototypes were completed but further development was discontinued.

ERF were busy in the early Sixties too, experimenting with alternative power units, transmissions and braking

Leyland's Gas Turbine

systems. Their 88R Rolls Royce petrol engined lightweight eight wheel tanker for Shell BP was announced in 1961. It was capable of well over 70 mph and had front disc brakes. One of these machines also operated with Proctor & Gamble on the transport of edible oils. The following year another eight wheeler with the new LV cab featured a Bristol Siddeley SRM fully automatic hydraulic torque converter gearbox and Eaton two-speed double drive rear bogie with Hendrickson air suspension. Girling disc brakes were fitted to both front axles.

Apart from such excursions into the unknown, the basic design of goods vehicles did not change dramatically. Weight, size and power all increased and a serious effort was made by most British manufacturers to improve cab comfort as drivers began to get a taste for the better appointed cabs fitted to some of the European imports.

As well as introducing tilt cabs for better engine access, such details as four headlamp systems, one piece wrap-round windscreens, lower entry steps and fully lined interiors with sound-proofing were appearing.

Hauliers were becoming more image conscious too. Features in trade magazines urged them to look at their vehicle liveries and freshen up their paint jobs. Unfortunately some companies with superb traditional liveries took their advice and replaced them with plain sterile treatments often using white and economising on lettering to the point of being anonymous. It was thought 'trendy' to remove all names and addresses and replace them with a design-conscious logo and no more.

One of the more familiar and best designed liveries, that of British Road Services, underwent change in the Sixties. When the BTC was wound up the attractive lion and wheel roundel went too and the merging of divisions under the THC gave rise to a new numbering system which was more difficult to understand than the very clear system used in the Fifties.

The Sixties will surely be remembered as one of the more turbulent decades in British transport. The transition from slow old fashioned lorries to higher powered European style artics is recorded here in pictures. Four sections look at four wheelers, six wheelers, eight wheelers and artics. The effects of change are obvious. In 1960 one could still see the last remnants of the old world but, by the end of the decade, the 'new broom' of legislation had swept it all away. We had moved into another new era of transport.

COMPARISON CHART – BEFORE AND AFTER 1964

The chart below shows typical examples of heavy goods vehicles built before and after the 1964 UK Construction & Use Regulations came into effect. The vehicles depicted here represent maximum GVW models from well known manufacturers. Pre 1964 four wheelers and rigid six wheelers were permitted a maximum length of 30ft. This was raised to 36ft after 1964. All figures given are based purely on nominal values and do not necessarily serve as accurate data for the vehicles shown.

Abbreviations:

GW – Gross Weight; **NP** – Nominal Payload; **BL** – Nominal Body/Trailer Length; **OL** – Overall Length; **PO** – Power Output

---

FOUR WHEELERS   Scale Approx 1 : 140

ERF 5.4G
1960

GW: 14 tons
NP: 9 tons
BL: 20ft
OL: 26ft
PO: 94 bhp

BEDFORD KMH
1966

GW: 16 tons
NP: 10 tons
BL: 22ft 6in
OL: 29ft 1in
PO: 146 bhp

SIX WHEELERS

THORNYCROFT MASTIFF
1960

GW: 20 tons
NP: 13.5 tons
BL: 21ft
OL: 27ft 6in
PO: 130 bhp

ATKINSON L2266X
1966

GW: 22 tons
NP: 15 tons
BL: 24ft
OL: 29ft 10in
PO: 150 bhp

EIGHT WHEELERS

LEYLAND OCTOPUS 24.O9
1961

GW: 24 tons
NP: 16 tons
BL: 24ft
OL: 30ft
PO: 140 bhp

FODEN 8E7/28
1966

GW: 28 tons
NP: 19 tons
BL: 30ft*
OL: 36ft*
PO: 225 bhp

* with platform body. Tipper shown.

ARTICS

BRISTOL HA6LL
1960

GW: 24 tons
NP: 15 tons
BL: 26ft
OL: 35ft
PO: 150 bhp

AEC MAMMOTH MINOR
1968

GW: 32 tons
NP: 20 tons
BL: 40ft
OL: 49ft 2in
PO: 226 bhp

FOUR WHE

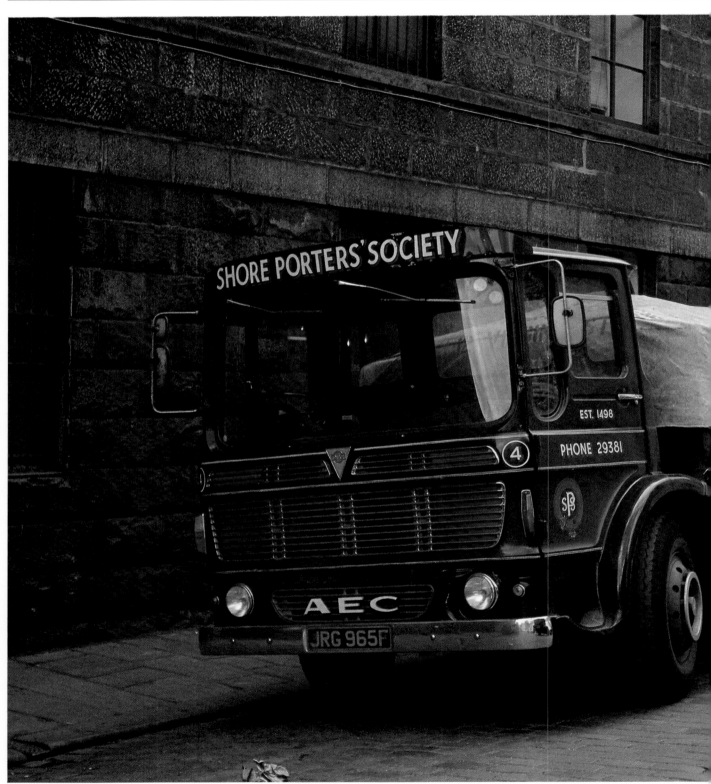

ELERS

As the basic workhorse of distribution fleets, parcels carriers, public utilities and local authorities the four wheeler represents the largest section of the lorry population. For years it had remained at 12 tons maximum gvw but in 1955 was allowed 14 tons. In 1964 the limit was raised again to 16 tons. The significant difference between the old 12 ton gvw models and the '16 tonners' was the load distribution. The 12 ton models had, in theory, an even 2-ton loading on each tyre (4-ton front/8-ton rear). This resulted in a well-balanced ratio of body length to wheelbase. The 14-ton models had a slightly less balanced front to rear split of 5 tons and 9 tons. When the 16-ton limit was allowed the rear axle loading was pegged at 10 tons while 6 tons was allowed on the front.

In order to avoid rear axle overloading a shorter rear overhang was required. This meant that the longest bodies required extra long wheelbases resulting in poorer turning circles. Power steering became a necessity. French regulations permit 19 tons gvw, split 6/13, which comes back nearer to the logical design giving even loadings on each tyre.

One effect of the 16-ton four wheelers coming in was that they took over the role of the old Chinese Six lorries of a similar gvw whose numbers rapidly diminished.

1968 16-ton gvw AEC Mercury with 'Ergomatic' tilt cab. With the introduction of this Leyland Group cab, AECs lost some of their individuality, although mechanically they were still entirely AEC. This example was photographed at the Aberdeen premises of the old established Shore Porters Society.

1. Just as Leyland influenced AEC styling in the mid Sixties so it had Albion's some years earlier. This 1960 Chieftain 10.75 ton gvw flat features the LAD (Leyland/Albion/Dodge) 'Vista View' cab launched in 1958. Leyland benefitted from Albion's engineering especially from their gearboxes and hub reduction axles. Sheffield-based J E Parker ran a mixed fleet of lorries on general haulage.

2. Albion's underfloor engined Claymore was launched in 1954, aimed at operators demanding a 3-seater cab such as in brewery and furniture removal fleets. It was powered by a horizontal version of Albion's 4.1 litre 4-cylinder diesel and had payload ratings of 4- or 5-tons. This one was photographed in the Derby area.

3. In 1964 Albions were given the Ergomatic cab making them hard to distinguish from Leylands and AECs. This Milk Marketing Board farm collection tanker is based on the 16-ton gvw 'Super Clydesdale' chassis.

4. From the cab design one could be excused for thinking this vehicle was an AEC Mandator. It is in fact one of a number of Duramin-cabbed Mercurys operated by the Express Dairy Co on transporting eggs from the West Country to London. A load consisted of up to 118000 eggs. It dates from 1961.

5. Making an interesting comparison with the Ergomatic-cabbed tanker opposite, this MMB Clydesdale is of the earlier 'LAD' 14-ton gvw type.

1

2

3

4

5

1

2

3

4

5

1. A 1964 Albion Claymore with a very stylish integral body, operated by Hector MacMillan Ltd of Burnham. The underfloor engined Claymore was produced between 1954 and 1964.

2. While many breweries operated the cheaper Bedfords, Fords and BMCs in their delivery fleets, John Smith of Tadcaster, Yorks had a number of heavy duty Atkinson drays powered by 4LW and 5LW Gardners and built on solid traditional lines.

3. Most large hauliers ran rigid or artic multi-wheelers on long distance work but sometimes four wheelers would be employed for loads of up to 10 tons. More often than not these were of the cheaper mass-produced variety so four wheel 'Atkis' like this one from the well-known Marshalls of Nottingham fleet were less common.

4. BRS Parcels, part of the THC (Transport Holding Company) from 1963 to 1969 and forerunner of the present-day NFC 'Lynx' express delivery network, were big enough to justify their own specially developed vehicle. Based on an Austin chassis it was built by group member Star Bodies of Oldham and produced in large numbers. It became affectionately known as the 'Noddy Van'.

5. Powered by the BMC 5.1 litre diesel this 1963 FFK140 represents Austin's biggest rigid vehicle of the period. This 7-ton flat belonged to Staffordshire haulier Wesson and carries the 'Staffordshire Knot' symbol on its doors in common with some other lorries from that area.

The four wheeler market was dominated by the mass-produced Bedford TK during the Sixties. This boxvan in British Road Services livery dates from 1963 and was photographed in the Bermondsey area. The whole street scene has been included if only for the interesting buildings and surrounding traffic which captures the atmosphere of the period.

1. An unusual cab built by Oldlands of Bristol adorns this 1960 AEC Mercury seen on pub deliveries of Badger Beers in Blandford Forum where brewers Hall and Woodhouse were based.

2. An example of the less common AEC Mandator Mk.V four wheeler which is not to be confused with the Mercury model. This higher powered long wheelbase drawbar model was only marketed in the UK from 1958 into the early Sixties. This Whitbread-liveried example photographed in Newcastle-on-Tyne dates from 1960.

3. A 1960 AEC Mercury Mk.II flat photographed near Edinburgh. This AV470-powered 9-tonner is in the livery of haulier F Bowker of Oldham and the differences between it and the Mandator pictured on the left are clearly apparent.

4. The Sixties saw many well-known brewers making bulk tanker deliveries to the larger pubs and hotels who had cellar tanks. This 1967 Austin FJK140 with a tank of approximately 40-barrel capacity was seen delivering to the Red Lion Hotel, Luton in February 1968.

1. Bedford TK, seen as a sensational new cab ahead of engine design when launched in 1960, came in a wide variety of weights and sizes. A short-lived variant, the 1.7 ton payload KA was added in 1965 but low sales volume saw its withdrawal only five years later. For its role it was over-cabbed and the established J1 35 cwt model did the same job more efficiently.

2. Haulage contractor J F Spicer of Hitchin operated this Bedford TJ 7-tonner on contract to Geo W King of Stevenage. The TJ was launched in 1958, successor to a long line of highly successful normal-control Bedfords dating back to the Thirties. The TJ was withdrawn from the UK market in 1975 but continued to be sold in Third World export markets. One of the longest running truck models of all time, the TJ is still in production at the AWD-Bedford plant in Dunstable.

3. A classic distribution role for the Bedford TK which set the standard for economical middle-weight trucks in the Sixties and Seventies. By 1978 over half a million had been sold worldwide. This one operated in the well-known SPD fleet and was based at their Chesham depot in Buckinghamshire.

4. Local dock haulier Pope & Sons found the TK suited to short haul operations around the old Port of London and Tilbury. TKs were half the price of some premium trucks but with their low unladen weight carried just as much payload. The TK easy entry cab gave improved comfort and spares were cheap and plentiful.

5. Even leading long distance fleets like that of tanker operator Harold Wood at Heckmondwyke near Bradford found a role for the TK, like this 1965 model.

1

2

3

4

5

1. In the late Sixties Austin and Morris truck models were badged 'BMC'. This 16-ton gvw Mastiff boxvan served in the H B Everton fleet based at Droitwich in the West Midlands and was on contract to the British Sugar Corporation at Kidderminster. By the early Seventies BMC models had become the Leyland Redline range.

2. 1960 Dennis Pax II tanker in the colours of fuel distributors Charrington Gardner and Lockett. The Pax was Dennis Brothers leading product powered mainly by Perkins. The late Fifties saw it offered with the more powerful 5.1 litre BMC 6-cylinder diesel.

3. Biggest rival to the Bedford TK was Ford's D series which appeared five years after the TK and replaced the dated Trader Mk.2. This example on 10-stud wheels is a 12-ton gvw 'D800' with bulk cement body from the large Cement Marketing Co 'Blue Circle' fleet.

4. In 1966, following on from new legislation permitting heavier weights, Bedford launched the 16-ton gvw KM. Based on the same concept as the TK it featured a completely new 466 cu.in. 6-cylinder diesel. The KM's appearance was made distinctive by its white double bumpers. Limited engine access was something of a drawback. This KMS tipper was operated on coal haulage by Walker Bros at Cowdenbeath.

1

4

2

3

1. Popular among tipper operators was the Commer CBDS715 7-ton payload model. Powered by the TS3 2-stroke diesel, this one was operated by A T Jenkins of Welwyn and was photographed on the A6 near Barton-le-Clay, Beds.

2. A fine selection of 'classic' cars, including an Imp, a Hunter and a Minx from Hillman plus a Singer Vogue, form the load for this Commer CBDS762 transporter from Rootes dealers Holmes & Smith of Southend-on-Sea. It was appearing at the Southend eliminating round of the Lorry Driver of the Year contest in 1964.

3. Barely identifiable as a Commer, is this solidly proportioned security van seen delivering at a Luton bank in 1967. It appears to be based on a Perkins-engined VA model.

4. Commer's Dunstable built 8-tonner, the CBEW8 was powered by their famous TS3 3-cylinder opposed piston 2-stroke diesel engine. This 1963 dropside lorry worked in the fleet of Skelton Transport of Timperley, Manchester.

5. Largest of the TS3 powered Commer range was the 'Maxiload' 16-ton gross introduced in 1964. E E Howe Transport of Enfield ran this long wheelbase CCGW1615 model with a traditionally built timber dropside body. The TS3 fitted in the 'Maxiload' developed 135 bhp.

1

2

4

5

A fine ERF drawbar outfit from Falkirk-based Gallin & Will. The LV-cabbed ERF is a true classic of the Sixties and this well turned out machine has been captured to good advantage as it heads south on the M6 motorway. Launched in 1962 the LV fibreglass cab continued to be fitted until the last A series in the mid Seventies. So durable was ERF's engineering that a number of LVs are still in daily use after more than 20 years service.

1

2

3

4

5

1. Not as common as other makes in the Sixties, Dennis still had a small share of the middleweight market. This Pax IV long wheelbase pantechnicon worked in the large fleet of Alston Bros Furniture which was based at Ipswich.

2. A striking new tilt cab graced the Dodge K '500 Series' when introduced in 1966. This example was among the first to be seen by the author and was brand new when photographed. It belonged to the Atlas Transport & Shipping Co of Battersea. Standard power unit was the Perkins 6.354, while the higher powered Chrysler V6 was optional.

3. A somewhat rare vehicle was the Dennis Stork. It was designed as a purpose-built 3-ton payload distribution vehicle with underfloor engine and low-step walk-through cab to compete with the Albion Claymore. This one, photographed delivering to a Luton hardware shop, bears the names 'E.P. Racing' and 'Ferrari' but the link between these and hardware is a little obscure.

4. Forerunner of the Dodge '500 Series', seen opposite, was the '300 Series'. This heavy duty D309/310 features the LAD cab similar to that used on the Leyland Comet. It is in British Road Services Ltd livery and operated from their Eastern Division.

5. This intriguing shot of a 1967 ERF 5.4G from the Midlands-based Birmid fleet, shows it to have non standard cast spoke wheels rarely seen on British vehicles. Birmid Ltd are leading suppliers of castings to the motor industry.

1. 1968 ERF 'LV' dropside operated by haulage contractors W Woodhall & Son of Coalport, Telford in Shropshire. This model was one of the most popular premium heavy duty four wheelers of the Sixties being light in weight and extremely economical.

2. Guy soon lost its famous Indian's Head motif after Jaguar took the company over in 1961. Instead a rather anonymous 'J' symbol appeared on the 'Big J' as the new 1964 range was called. 'Big Js' featured the Motor Panels cab shared with some Seddon, Foden, Scammell and ERF models and a wide choice of power units was offered. For solo 16-ton gvw operation the popular choice was either the AEC AV505 at 149 bhp or the 138 bhp O.401 Leyland. This vehicle served in the well-known Smith of Maddiston fleet.

3. For specialised low loading height duties such as soft drinks distribution and manually loaded dustcarts, the humble Karrier Bantam was a highly successful machine. The marque was originally introduced in the early Thirties and remained in use until 1978. This 1960 example is from the Corona Soft Drinks fleet and was used on shop and house to house deliveries.

4. Edinburgh-based Forth Haulage Co operated this fine 1962 14-ton gvw KV-cabbed ERF 5.4G flat which was photographed in London's Silvertown area. The KV ('Kleer-View') cab only survived into the early Sixties as 1962 saw the launch of the new LV-cabbed range which was mechanically similar.

5. Another example of Guy's 'Big J4' – a 1967 dropside lorry from Walsall-based J F Lycett. Like the majority of 'Big J4s' on 16-ton operation, it would have been powered by either an AV505 or an O.401. Heavier models for trailer operation had the further choice of Gardner and Cummins units ranging from 180 to 212 bhp.

1

2

3

4

5

1

2

1. Launched in 1962 as a rival to Bedford's popular TJ model, Ford's NC Trader did not achieve the same worldwide popularity. This 4-ton furniture van is from Pickford's Removal fleet and bears the fleet number M3528. A choice of 4-cylinder petrol or diesel engines was offered, the most common being the 220 cu.in. 4D diesel.

2. The Milk Marketing Board (now Dairy Products Transport) switched to Fords in the mid Fifties. This 1961 6D diesel-powered Trader in the old dark green and white livery was based at Felinfach creamery in West Wales. Churn collection was phased out in 1979, the role being carried out more efficiently by new bulk tankers of the type shown on pages 14 & 15.

3. Having become firmly 'bogged down' on a tricky site the driver of this 1965 short wheelbase Trader 7-ton tipper prepares to summon the 'drot' to pull him out of trouble.

4. These days AWD is associated with Bedford's Dunstable truck plant which was taken over by David J B Brown in 1986. There is no connection with this AWD, namely All-Wheel-Drive of Camberley, Surrey who specialised in building 4x4 and 6x6 conversions in the late Fifties and Sixties. They were mainly based on Ford Thames Traders as is this example, one of two spreaders seen at the Breedon and Cloud Hill Lime Works near Derby. AWD became part of the Vickers Group.

5. For the short period between 1965 and 1969 International Harvester set up a truck building operation in Doncaster, Yorks to produce a range of medium weight trucks tailored to the UK market. These anglicised Internationals never sold in large volume but they appeared in a number of roles as trucks, tippers and artics. Under their bonnets they had the Perkins 6.354 diesel. This one dating from 1967 was in the service of the British and Foreign Wharf Co of London.

1. Foden four wheelers were not as numerous as some makes, the bulk of their sales being in the rigid six, rigid eight and artic class. One company that used them was the famous engine manufacturer, Gardner. This 1968 example has the S36 style cab.

2. A distinctive livery worth recording was that of J Lyons & Co. Here it adorns a mid Sixties Morris FGK40 boxvan with the 'angle planned' safety cab.

3. A 1968 Ergomatic-cabbed Leyland Super Comet with boxvan body seen delivering in the West Wales coastal resort of Aberystwyth. It was operated by Hills Transport of Cardiff.

4. This attractive Thames Trader removal van in the livery of P Chaplin of Colwyn Bay, North Wales dates from 1963.

5. A G Maidment & Sons Ltd, the meat haulage specialists from Tisbury near Shaftesbury in Wiltshire, operated this 1968 Guy 'Big J4' fitted with refrigerated van bodywork.

1

2

3

4

5

1

2

3

4

1. Like certain Albion and Dodge vehicles depicted earlier in this section, the Leyland CS3 Comet featured the LAD cab. This short wheelbase tipper operated in the well-known General Refractories fleet from Sheffield and was engaged on transporting industrial sands.

2. Less common among Leylands was the '90' model having yet another variant of the LAD cab. This 1965 model grossed at 4.5 tons and was powered by the OE.160 4-cylinder 60 bhp diesel. It competed with such machines as the Austin/ Morris/BMC 'FG' series, which were themselves absorbed into the Leyland Group in 1968. Introduced in 1963 and built at the Standard Triumph plant they were originally powered by the OE.138 54 bhp diesel and simply known as the '2-tonner'.

3. Many types of operation require large volume vans with low floor and full width cab, seating extra crew members. The underfloor-engined Leyland Tiger Cub coach chassis formed a good basis for such vans. This 1967 'Luton' is an excellent example operated by Thomas Eastham & Son, the kitchen unit specialist from Blackpool, Lancs.

4. When the Leyland Ergomatic cab began appearing on AECs and Albions as well as their own range it became difficult to tell them apart at first glance but chassis details such as fuel tanks, exhausts and hubs were easily identifiable, not to mention the minor variations in grilles and badging. This 1968 Super Comet flat is seen in the grey, dark blue and red livery of Holt Lane Transport from Prescot, whose main work was the transport of BICC cables.

1. The author braved a heavy rainstorm to get this shot of a 1967 Leyland '90' boxvan ploughing through floods on the southern outskirts of Luton in 1968.

2. A typical example of the Morris FGK40 'angle planned' 2-tonner. Originally launched in 1961 the manufacturers made much of the revolutionary cab shape which eventually earned it the nickname 'Threepenny Bit' after the multi-sided coin in use at that time. A choice of 4-litre 6-cylinder petrol or 3.4 and 4-litre 4-cylinder diesel engines was offered. Its constant mesh gearbox was not so easy to handle for inexperienced drivers.

3. 1963 Morris FFK140 7-tonner with a very workmanlike wooden tipping body. This 5.1 litre diesel-engined machine was operated by H C Janes, the Luton-based building company. An optional higher powered 5.7 litre diesel was also available.

4. 1964 saw the introduction of one of the first mass-produced tilt-cab trucks in the UK – the 'FJ' series from Austin/ Morris. This FJK140 lwb 7-tonner was brand new in the fleet of J Lyons & Co and featured a newly introduced livery.

5. In the Sixties Scammell was one company who did not offer a normal road-going four wheeler, concentrating instead on eight wheelers and artics. However, they produced a wide variety of specialised off-road trucks of which this 1964 registered 'Mountaineer' 4x4 dumper is a typical example. It worked for the National Coal Board and was based in the Fife area of Scotland.

1

2

3

4

5

1

2

1. The Seddon Diesel '12-4' (12-ton gvw four wheeler) was a 7.5-ton payload model powered by a choice of Leyland '370' or Perkins '6.534' 6-cylinder diesel engines. A 14-ton ('14-4') version on 10-stud wheels was also offered featuring the Leyland '400' or Gardner 6LW power units. This BRS flat with its load of Goodyear tyres was based at Wolverhampton.

2. Another Seddon Diesel '12-4', this time a 'Luton' van from the London depot of B G Transport Service Ltd. The longest available wheelbase was 14ft.

3. A Leyland O.350 Comet diesel engine would have powered this Seddon Diesel dropside '7-tonner' dating from 1960. It was based at British Road Services, Dunstable Branch.

4. A new range of Seddons was introduced in 1964. Typical is this '13:Four' of Edward Sykes, Ashton-under-Lyne. Power came from the Perkins 6.354 6-cylinder diesel and the smart new cab was by Motor Panels.

5. Though not a load carrying vehicle this 1964 4x4 timber tractor has been included to represent the products of Unipower Ltd who were based at Perivale in Middlesex. Named the 'Hannibal' it was fitted with a Gardner 5LW oil engine.

3

4

5

SIX W

The new 22-ton gvw six wheelers from 1964 provided as much payload capacity as the early Fifties rigid eights at 15 tons. Six wheelers of under 18ft outer axle spread were limited to 20 tons and these were mainly confined to tipping duties or for use as readymix vehicles.

Conversion specialists like the Primrose Third Axle Co, the York Third Axle Co, Henry Boys, Unipower and Reynolds Boughton produced large numbers of six wheelers based on standard four wheel chassis, mainly from Austin, Bedford, Commer, Dodge and Morris. These were often designed for lower gross weights.

Twin steers or 'Chinese Sixes' lost some popularity being limited to 17/18 tons gvw. One type of six wheeler which became more common in the Sixties was the special low loading platform type used on brewery work.

Seen on Glasgow Docks near Finnieston Quay is this classic example of British haulage vehicles from the Sixties. Feather & Kent of Colne were an old established Lancashire haulage company. The vehicle is an AEC Marshal dating from 1968 and powered by the AV505 146 bhp 6-cylinder diesel. This part of the Glasgow scene disappeared when the area was redeveloped for the Garden Festival and the construction of the Scottish Exhibition Centre. In the Sixties it was still full of interest with ocean-going cargo ships and dock cranes towering over the quayside, forming a perfect backdrop for any working lorry.

HEELERS

1

2

1. 1965 'GM6R' Marshal – one of the last Park Royal style AEC light six wheelers prior to the introduction of Leyland's Ergomatic cab. This lorry, seen here when new, was operated by Firth Cleveland Fastenings Ltd of Treforest in South Wales.

2. One of the most common and most successful six wheelers of its era was the Albion Reiver. This one, operated by G Pickett & Son of Wordsley for E J & J Pearson Ltd, was beautifully painted in a traditional dark blue and red with gold lettering. It carried the fleet name 'Hearts Delight' on the front panel. Instead of the usual newspaper or sack over the radiator it had a purpose-made upper 'muff' – an accessory not often bothered with. It dates from 1963.

3. A superbly liveried 1961 Reiver reflects the glare of the afternoon sun as it passes through St Neots on the old A1 trunk road. The livery is that of Pollock of Musselburgh who operate one of the best turned out fleets in the country.

3

4. Rounding Hyde Park Corner in the thick of London's traffic is a 1962 Austin FFK140 six wheel dropside. Typical of the many third axle conversions carried out on low cost mass-produced chassis, it came from the Potteries-based Longton and North Staffs fleet in Fenton.

5. Tilt-cab Austin 'FJ' with third axle conversion, possibly by Primrose who were the leading specialists. With its heavy wooden dropside body and seagull pattern rear wings it presents a very impressive appearance. Haulier A. Welch of West Bromwich operated this handsome machine on the transport of road springs for Richard Berry & Sons.

4

5

1. A load of sheep crosses Shap summit in the afternoon sunshine. Their conveyance is a 1962 Atkinson L1266 with a triple deck livestock body, registered 95GAO.

2. A very unusual six wheeler is this Bedford Primrose-based J6L powered by Bedford's '300' 90 bhp diesel. Having a decidedly foreign appearance with its large tilt body, it served in the Wellingborough-based fleet of Whitworths Foods. The signwriting advertises Whitworths Champion Self Raising Flour. It is built on a mean wheelbase of 17ft 2in.

3. With a strident blast from its forward-facing exhaust, a Commer-Unipower type TS3-powered six wheel tipper out-accelerates a little Riley Elf from traffic lights on the old A1 at Biggleswade. This 1965 'CC8'-based machine belonged to Lowe Bros of Middleton in Teesdale, Co. Durham.

4. 1961 Atkinson L1266 20-ton gvw six wheeler powered by a Gardner 6LX oil engine developing 150 bhp. It belonged to the large fleet of Tayforth Group member, Road Services Caledonian. Firmly chained down on to its platform body is a demountable bulk tank for the transport of liquid synthetic adhesive.

5. Taking a break at the Wharf car park in Newark-on-Trent, this generously bodied coke tipper dates from 1961. It is one of many third axle conversions carried out by specialists like the Primrose Third Axle Co and York Third Axles. This one is based on the 7.5-ton payload Bedford KG model with its Leyland 350 cu.in. Comet engine. It is in the orange and black livery of Walter Woodthorpe from Boston Dock.

1

2

3

4

5

2

3

1. This 1966 AEC Marshal 'Ergomatic' had done very little work when photographed near Ruislip, Middlesex. It is in the sober livery of Indestructo Glass who were a contract customer of British Road Services.

2. A less common axle configuration is featured on this Regent Petroleum tanker. It is a 1965 AEC Mercury with Primrose 'Rear-a-Steer' second axle conversion and was one of a number built for that company on a mixture of AEC Mercury and Guy Warrior chassis.

3. 1968 saw the introduction of Bedford's own factory-built 22-ton gvw six wheeler, the HRX3 or 'KME' powered by the 466 cu.in. 6-cylinder Bedford diesel. It was of the single-drive 'trailing axle' type with 4-spring bogie. This example was photographed in London and is mounted with a lift-off refrigerated meat container. The operators were Sunderland-based C B Chastney Ltd.

4. While ERF forward control 'KV' cabbed lorries were common, semi-forward versions were few and far between. This distinctive design with its bulbous, protruding front became known as the 'Sabrina' after the shapely female showbiz personality of that name. Some entered service with breweries where extra crew accommodation was required. This machine served in the large Rotherham-based fleet of Leonard Green who were engaged on steel haulage. It dates from 1960.

1

4

1. Depicting a 1967 Bedford KM with third axle conversion, this colour shot has been reproduced if only to record the superb livery of its operators J Beasley, an old established traditional style East London haulier.

2. Low cost mass-produced trucks were sometimes elevated to the status of 'premium' long distance heavies by the addition of extra axles and a richly designed paint scheme. This 1965 Ford Thames Trader is one such machine from Dundee-based D & D Haulage and was photographed passing through Newcastle-on-Tyne, loaded to the 'gunnels'.

3. Beaumont Steeplejacks from South West London operated this unusual ERF six wheeler fitted with a neatly designed crew cab version of the 'LV'. It dates from 1965.

4. Another popular practice to increase payload capacity on four wheelers was the conversion to 'Chinese Six' by adding a second steering axle. Such conversions were usually the work of Blackburn-based Primrose Third Axle Co. This is a particularly good example based on a Commer CC8 2-stroke and used by the Alston Foundry Co for the haulage of moulding sand.

5. Well-known printers Samuel Jones of St Neots were the operators of this impressive large capacity boxvan based on a 1966 Dodge K900 six wheeler. It features the tilt cab launched in that year.

1

2

3

4

1

2

3

4

5

1. The Dodge T300 series was a solidly built six wheeler powered by a choice of AEC AV470 (T310) or Perkins 6.354 (T308). This one, built in 1964, features the LAD cab and worked in the Essex-based fleet of A J Brush Ltd of Maldon.

2. A newly delivered 1966 Foden 'S21' (nicknamed the 'Mickey Mouse') six wheeler waits to go to work at its owner's premises, the Ambergate works of wire manufacturers Richard Johnson & Nephew. The heavily-built timber body has no less than 17 close-spaced cross-bearers to withstand the heavy point loadings of the wire coils.

3. Hauliers P Partrick & Son of Wellingborough operated this smart 'LV'-cabbed ERF Chinese Six flat dating from 1962. At 16-ton gvw (5LW) and 17-ton (6LW) these ERFs could carry legal payloads of approximately 10 – 11 tons – one or two tons more than a 14-ton gvw four wheeler. The post '64 16-ton gvw rating for four wheelers robbed any advantage from this class of twin steer and they were gradually phased out.

4. The late Sixties saw a number of Guy 'Big J' six and eight wheelers entering the Post Office Supplies Department fleet, replacing their AEC and Maudslay vehicles from the Fifties. This 22-ton gross example is typical of their heavily-built dropside trucks.

5. Low loading heights demanded by brewery crews brought about a new breed of six wheeler with 16in. wheels. This 1965 Dennis Pax V illustrates the point. Bedford, Ford and BMC were also big producers of these special distribution vehicles. They grossed around 16 tons. This Dennis is in the pale yellow livery of Flowers Brewery who were part of the Whitbread Group.

1. This late Foden FG6/12 'S20' of London & Welsh Transport bearing a 1963 registration is perhaps more typical of the Fifties. It looks quite dated next to the 'S21' cabbed models of the period. It carries an equally old style demountable insulated container.

2. In its striking red livery this Gardner-powered Camerons Brewery Seddon six wheeled tanker grossed 20 tons. Seddon six and eight wheelers featured the 'Maxartic' rear bogie, an advanced design of two-spring arrangement having tapered leaf springs.

3. Thornycroft road vehicle production was phased out early in the decade after the company became part of the ACV Group. This Mastiff six wheeler was one of the last important models, announced in November 1959. It was dubbed the 'Express Freighter' and was capable of speeds of over 60 mph to suit motorway operation. The 130 bhp QR6 6-cylinder diesel was fitted and the vehicle was designed for 20-tons gvw. This 1960 flat is in the colours of Hulland Products from Hulland Ward, Derby.

4. Except for a few 'one-off' specials, Scammell did not offer rigid six wheelers in the Sixties, concentrating on heavy tractors and off-road vehicles. Representing Scammell's products is this massive 240-ton gtw 6x4 'Contractor' heavy haulage tractor coupled to a 300-ton capacity 12-axle Crane Fruehauf girder frame trailer. The tractor is PGO711E, Pickford's fleet number M4944. Power came from a 335 bhp Cummins diesel.

1

2

3

1

2

1. Although Leyland had launched their LAD-cabbed 'Power Plus' range which included a new Hippo six wheeler, an odd example of its mid Fifties predecessor continued to appear like this one registered in March 1961. It ran in the fleet of H B & H (Transport) Ltd of Newton-le-Willows. A new 'Power Plus' Octopus is visible in the background making an interesting comparison of the two cab designs.

2. Seddon Diesel offered a wide range of power options and gvw ratings on their Mk.2 six wheeler models launched in 1962. GVWs of 16, 17, 18 and 20-tons were available, all except the 20-ton model being on 8-stud wheels. Perkins 6.354 or Leyland 370 and 400 engines were available. The heaviest models took the 400 Leyland or a choice of Gardner 5LW, 6LW or 6LX. This example from Athersmith Bros has 8-stud wheels and single-drive so it would probably be a '16-6' grossing 16 tons. All had the 'Maxartic' tapered leaf 2-spring rear bogie.

3

3. Forerunner of the Mk.2 Seddon six wheeler was the Mk.l5/10 trailing axle 17-ton gvw model (18 tons with 10.00x20 front tyres) powered by the Leyland '375' diesel. It was light, having a chassis/cab kerb weight of only 5.2 tons. T A Metcalfe of Darlington operated this flat which dates from the beginning of January 1960.

4. International Harvester's Doncaster-built 'Loadstar' range included a bonneted rigid six wheeler seen here in tipper form in the livery of W H Poxon Haulage from Newthorpe near Leeds.

5. A fine example of Thornycroft's Mastiff 6x2 Express Freighter described on p.57. This was one of a number operated by Merrall's Transport of Egham, Surrey.

4

5

EIGHT

Until the Sixties eight wheelers were the leading long distance heavies in Britain but they lost ground when the law changed in 1964 permitting longer and heavier artics. The remainder of the decade saw a steady fall in demand for rigid eights. Leyland, one of the leading producers historically, even pulled out of the eight wheeler market altogether, to return in the mid Seventies after 30 tons was allowed on four axles.

Under the 1964 regulations 28 tons gvw was allowed on eight wheelers but only on an impossibly long outer axle spread of 26ft, which made them difficult to manoeuvre. In consequence very few were built at this weight. However, many operators still chose to run rigid eights at 24 and 26 tons for tipper and tanker applications.

Last of a long line of pure-bred AEC eight wheelers, and arguably one of the finest examples of the breed, was the Mk.V Mammoth Major. Originally launched in 1958 it remained in production until 1965 when it was replaced by the Ergomatic-cabbed TG8RA models which were designed for 24 and 26 tons gross operation to take advantage of the new 1964 weight limits. The Mk.V shown here operated in the large AEC fleet of Spiers of Melksham in Wiltshire.

WHEELERS

1

2

3

4

1. Featuring 40x8 wheel and tyre equipment which died out in the Sixties, this John Wyatt contract vehicle from the Rothwell, Leeds based tanker fleet of Smith & Robinson Ltd is an AEC Mk.V dating from 1962.

2. Mainstay of many long distance haulage fleets, the AEC Mk.V is remembered as the archetypal British 'heavy' of the early Sixties pre-artic era. This example registered in 1965, near the end of the Mk.V's production period, operated with William Nuttall & Sons Ltd of Clifton, Manchester, whose regular customers included the famous 'Exide' and 'Chloride' battery manufacturers Electric Power Storage of Clifton.

3. Seen here with a 16-ton load of engineering bricks this G8RAD was well suited to the hilly areas of its native West Wales – it had the higher powered 11.3 litre engine. It also featured a 'Harold Wood' cab. It is seen here at Cynghordy in South Wales with bricks destined for sewer construction at the new Vauxhall car factory in Ellesmere Port, Merseyside.

4. Meat and fish hauliers Claben Ltd of Aberdeen were the operators of this 1965 Mk.V 'reefer' seen heading down the Great North Road at 'full song'.

5. 1962 Park Royal cabbed 24-ton gvw 4000-gal tanker in the livery of Jet Petroleum. The AEC Mk.V was used widely in this role by nearly all the leading fuel distribution fleets.

5

1. Another Mk.V flat in the naturally 'matured' condition that lorries develop after some years service. It is seen fully loaded with sheet steel and belonged to M J Parry of Bayston Hill, Shropshire, the bulk of whose traffic consisted of livestock.

2. A popular choice for most large tanker operators, the Mk.V could be seen in almost every well-known livery. These included Harold Wood, Smith & Robinson, Wincanton Transport, Pickfords, James Hemphill and, in this instance, John Forman of Hull.

3. Contrasting with the dignified lines of the Mk.V, the new Leyland-inspired 'Ergomatic' presented a 'fussier' appearance, typical perhaps of Sixties styling and pressed steel construction. This 1968 TG8R is in the livery of S P & G C Kidman of Hail Weston, Huntingdon.

4. 1969 short wheelbase bulk tanker of Hall & Co (Thames Valley) Ltd, part of the RMC Group. Note how the driving mirrors on this and the previous 'Ergo' are mounted on the 'A' pillar and viewed through the windscreen. Earlier models had door mounted mirrors like the BRS example shown below.

5. A well-laden 1967 BRS 'Ergo' Mammoth Major carrying long steel girders, the rear ends of which are supported on a 2-axle 'dolly'.

1

2

3

4

2

3

1

1. Long after introducing their 'Mk.1' cab with wrap-round screen, Atkinson still supplied their coachbuilt 'bow front' cab which originally appeared in the mid Fifties. This Gardner 6LX powered L1786XA was registered as late as 1963. It served in the well-known fleet of McPhee's (Newcastle) Ltd and features 40x8 tyres.

2. Although earlier than the McPhee's vehicle shown above, this L1786, also on 40x8s, is fitted with the 'wrap-round' cab. The decorative headboard displays an elephant's head and the words 'Hull & London Nightly Trunk Service'. E Brown & Sons were based at Queensgate Filling Station, Beverley in East Yorkshire.

3. Dating from 1964 this 24-ton gvw Atkinson L1786XA would still have been the most efficient type of bulk tipper as the benefits of the new 32-ton artics and 28-ton rigids had not quite come into being. Atkinson had by this time introduced the Mk.1 cab with four headlamp system but this one, belonging to Roberts Transport of Knighton in Radnorshire (now Powys), still featured the earlier two headlamp style.

4. A year later than the Roberts eight wheeler, this Suttons L2686XT tipping bulk powder tanker on contract to ICI Mond Division was built to conform with the 23ft outer axle spread required for operation at 26-tons gross.

4

The vehicles on this colour spread all have one thing in common – they have survived in preservation. Three have even retained their most important assets – their correct liveries.

1. Part of the well-known Craddock Bros fleet from Coven near Wolverhampton, this hard-worked 1962 L1786 Atkinson eight wheeled flat soldiered on in service for 20 years. When this shot was taken it was just over 11 years old. The lorry has been preserved but Craddock's livery, a true classic of the Sixties, has been lost.

2. Notable as the first Cummins-powered ERF built, ONH567 served in the fleet of C Butt of Northampton for 14 years. It's NH180 was something of a departure from ERF's normal practice, most of their production still being centred on Gardner engines. This photograph was taken in 1973. The 1961 vehicle is now, in 1991, undergoing restoration and will appear in its original operator's colours.

3. This 1963 'S20' cabbed Foden was one of a number specially built for the London-based Albion Sugar Co. It features a fully enclosed glucose tank built by W P Butterfield of Shipley, Yorks. The photograph was taken while it was still at work in 1971. After lying derelict for some years it was restored to original in 1984 and still survives in its correct livery.

4. This superb machine has already been featured on the Preface pages of this book. This colour shot dates from 1971. The AEC triangle reads AF (Alan Firmin) and the AF105 registration is characteristic of the company's fleet in that era. 'AF' is an early Cornish mark. The vehicle, a 'G8RAD', was cut down into a recovery vehicle when it left the haulage scene and survived in that role until Alan Firmin Transport decided to restore the lorry back to original condition. It was completed in 1991.

5. One of the more memorable colour schemes was that of Aaron Henshall from Hope Street, Prescot, Liverpool. The company was bought out by Holt Lane Transport, also of Prescot. Many of the old Henshall fleet of Atkinson and Leyland eight wheeler and trailer outfits were withdrawn from service while some of Holt Lane's large Atkinson eight wheeler fleet were transferred into the Henshall colours. 788WTE was one, seen here in the idyllic setting of Liverpool Docks in 1974. It has survived but in a fictitious livery.

1

2

3

4

5

1

2

3

1. Traditional 24-ton gross long wheelbase eight wheeled bulk tipper from the fleet of Hargreaves Motors Ltd of Rothwell near Leeds, photographed on the approach to the Runcorn Widnes Bridge.

2. 1963 L1786 in the inimitable colour scheme of Pollock of Musselburgh. 3722SC, fleet name 'Two Capitals', has the four headlamp system. Note that the headlamps and the twin foglamps have chromed 'eyebrows', a popular 'bolt on' item in the Sixties. This vehicle has also survived, restored to its correct livery.

3. Bearing a 1964 registration mark ARB473B, this 24-ton gross 'KV' cabbed rigid eight dropside of Sheffield-based Riley's Transport must have been one of the very last to enter service as the new 'LV' cabbed models had already been on the market for two years.

4. One of the best known names in tank haulage appears on this superb 'LV'cabbed 6.8GX3 ERF registered in 1965. Fleet No. 193 from Smith & Robinson of Oulton Lane, Rothwell, Leeds is among the last of the truly traditional 24-ton gross machines which present a very 'balanced' appearance. Powered by a Gardner '150' it has eight wheel brakes and a flat 21in. four-spoke steering wheel reminiscent of the old Fifties era.

4

1. This 1961 'KV' cabbed 6.8GX in the livery of Cerebos Foods Ltd was photographed in the Derby area. With its 24ft body and sheeted load it belonged very much to the old era.

2. One year older, this 6.8GX bears another famous name – Reliance Motors (Sale) Ltd who were the very first to use an ERF eight wheeler when that company built the original 'CI6.8' in 1934. Note that the fuel tank is right hand mounted, an arrangement often seen on tankers so that the left hand chassis side was clear to group the tank outlets.

3. The earliest pattern of 'LV' cab, developed by Bowyer Bros of Congleton, appears on this 6.8GX of Ken Evans of Gnosall, Staffordshire. The large white 'ERF' letters appear to have been added and the original badge (as illustrated on the right) is missing. Vertically mounted push-button door handles and a full width hinged front access panel are early features.

4. For comparison this 1964 'LV' cabbed 6.8GX bulk flour tanker has the smaller front access panel and horizontal door handles. It was photographed near Ollerton, Yorks and was painted in the red and cream livery of Thomas Sugden & Son Ltd, the Brighouse-based flour millers.

1

2

1

2

4

1. A later version of the ERF 'LV' 6.8GX dating from 1968 has the modern 'ERF' badging and increased-area cooling grilles. This short wheelbase 24-ton gvw tipper served in the fleet of sand and ballast merchants L G Bradshaw & Sons of Barton, near Luton, and is equipped with super-single tyres at the rear.

2. The 'S20' cabbed 24-ton gvw model just survived into the early Sixties and this example, registered in 1960, has an old style U-section body and was operated on sand and ballast by Dagenham-based George Batten Ltd.

3. Even later, and featuring a very similar pattern of bodywork, is this 1962 machine belonging to Henry Winfield Ltd of Hemel Hempstead. Note the vertically mounted spare wheel in the only practical position for such an ultra short wheelbase of 13ft 6.5in (listed as 9ft 9.5in by Fodens as they alone chose to measure it from the second axle instead of the first).

4. Successor to the 'S20' was the 'S21' or 'Mickey Mouse' as it is widely known. Initially it was nicknamed the 'Sputnik' on account of its rotund shape. This 1962 tanker appears in the bright yellow livery of the Italian 'Agip' petrol company – a brand which was marketed briefly in the UK during the Sixties.

5. This handsomely liveried high-sided tipper in the maroon livery of H Evers Ltd from Ancoats, Manchester, features the 'S24' tilt-cab of 1962. Fodens were the first manufacturer to introduce tilt-cabs, a trend quickly followed by many others during the Sixties. This vehicle was new in 1964.

3

1. The Albion Sugar Co, referred to on page 68, continued to use Foden tankers well into the Seventies but the last ones to have the fully streamlined bodywork were 'S24s' like this one from 1967. The taped-up grille is possibly a draught excluding measure!

2. So typical of a damp wintry scene is this shot of a 1966 'Mickey Mouse' with its makeshift radiator blind. The driver sets about tidying the sheet on his load of paper reels. The lorry is in the livery of Manchester-based Joseph Hoyle but, as the headboard and registration number suggest, was originally liveried as 'Richard Johnson & Nephew', the wire manufacturers.

3. The Guy Invincible only survived until the mid Sixties, when the 'Big J' range came in. The Cement Marketing Co ran both types and this example is a 1964 Invincible short wheelbase bulker with twin 'Portasilo' type tanks. Unlike the 'Big J' this vehicle proudly bears its Indian's head. Quite often, as in this case, a driver or painter has patiently coloured in the ornate motif.

4. Looking pristine, as one might expect of a brand new vehicle, this 1968 ERF 6.8GX tanker with 'LV' cab had just entered service when photographed in Luton. It is in the attractive livery of Nafta Petroleum and is powered by the usual '150' Gardner 6LX.

5. One look at the high-sided body of this eight wheeled Foden tipper tells you that it was employed on coal and coke haulage. Based at Donisthorpe near Measham in Leicestershire, M Orpwood ran a fine fleet. This Gardner-powered 'S24' dates from 1963.

1

2

3

4

1

2

1. Illustrating Foden's many cab variants in the early Sixties here is a 1962-registered short wheelbase tipper with 'S21' Mickey Mouse cab. Its contemporaries visible in the Breedon and Cloud Hill Lime Works' yard include an 'S20' and an 'S34'.

2. An excellent example of the early Sixties 'Mk.2' Invincible from Guy Motors' factory in Fallings Park, Wolverhampton. This well-laden 24-ton gvw flat is from the Birmingham fleet of E & J Davis and is a 1962 model.

3. Foden were one of the first, and one of the few, to build a 28-ton gvw rigid eight on the ridiculously long 26ft outer axle spread required under the new 1964 Construction & Use Regulations. This was the same as the axle spread required for a 28-ton artic. Under the 1972 regulations the axle spread for this weight was reduced by over 6ft, permitting vehicles of less unwieldy proportions. This 'S24' cabbed tipper of Southport Sand dates from 1965 and has the 4.8 litre 6-cylinder 2-stroke engine.

4. An impressive Gardner 6LX 150-powered Guy 'Big J8' trailing axle eight wheeled 'reefer' in the service of the British Beef Co of Middlesbrough.

5. Passing an extraordinary piece of modern architecture in the City of Portsmouth is a 1968 Guy 'Big J8' petrol tanker of the Shell Mex and BP group delivery service.

3

4

1. This unusual Guy Warrior 'Light 8' has a dual purpose body. Basically a high-sided bulk tipper, it is shown in use here as a flat platform. A vertically mounted spare wheel was located on the nearside. It dates from 1961 and was powered by the AEC 'AV470' diesel.

2. One of the Post Office Supplies Department's fleet of Guy 'Big J8s' loaded with pipes and in the old red livery which was to disappear in the late Sixties when the fleet took on the new bright yellow colour scheme. This is a 1966 vehicle.

3. An LAD-cabbed 'Power Plus' Leyland Octopus pulls out of Tunnel Cement's Clyde works, its twin Portasilo type tanks heavily laden. This well proportioned short (14ft 9in) wheelbase bulker dates from 1963 and is in the dark green and red livery of W B Russell of Glasgow.

4. While the new 'Power Plus' Octopus launched in September 1960 had a heavy specification and a corresponding unladen weight, the new lightweight '24.LWO.1AR' of 1963 was half a ton lighter. It was 6in shorter in the wheelbase at 16ft 6in and featured the lighter duty Albion Reiver rear axles. It was also planned to make the plastic LAD cab standard. This 1964 'lightweight' worked in the Sutherlands of Peterhead fleet.

5. A 1962 'Power Plus' on the 17ft wheelbase. This is the heavier '240.9AR' version with the heavy duty Group rear axles which were scaled-up versions of the Albion hub-reduction type. A choice of engines, the 200 bhp O.680 or 140 bhp O.600, was offered.

1

2

3

4

5

1. A 1964 'lightweight' Octopus in operation as a bulk tanker for Castrol Industrial Oils. Its hinged access flap for the radiator filler appears to have been left open from its last 'top up'.

2. 'Power Plus' Octopus in its truly intended role as a top weight trailer outfit. This 1964 model carries the livery of Aaron Henshall of Prescot and is loaded here with empty returnable stillages destined for the Triplex factory in St Helens.

3. The relatively short-lived 'LAD' gave way to a new breed of Octopus in 1965. This was the 24OT/26OT range (T meaning the Ergomatic Tilt cab). At this stage Leyland made their first venture into the 26-ton gvw eight wheeler bracket with a longer wheelbase of 20ft 9in.

4. The shorter Octopus at 24 tons gvw continued to be offered but the 'Ergos' did not distinguish between haulage and tippers. Their wheelbases were commonised at 15ft 9in. This shot shows a 1967 model mounted with a tipping tank in the colours of British Industrial Sand Ltd.

5. For comparison this is an application more normally associated with longer wheelbase chassis – a smart tanker, also on the 15ft 9in wheelbase, in the livery of Major Petroleum of Hull. This dates from 1968. By 1970 Leyland had pulled out of the eight wheeler business and the 'Octopus' name lay dormant until revived in 1975 by the new 'Octopus 2'.

1

2

3

4

5

1. 1964 Leyland 24.09AR 'Power Plus' flat – a classic example of the short-lived breed in an equally classic livery, that of James Lynch from Northwich, Cheshire. The setting is Regent Road, Bootle.

2. Scammell eight wheelers, like this Routeman II seen in Hull Docks, stayed at 24-ton gvw until the 1972 regulations permitted 30 tons on four axles and 26 tons on the 'old' 24-ton axle spread.

3. This 1967 Routeman II flat belonging to Liverpool haulier T E & J Bramham is unusual in featuring a lift up fourth axle. Traction problems on the early Routeman II, which was only available as a single-drive model, led Scammell to offer an air load-transfer package in the early Sixties.

4. A perfect example of the 15ft 9in wheelbase 'Ergo' Octopus in the role of a short wheelbase tipper. This coal bulker with its enormous 'greedy' board extensions grossed 24 tons and is in the livery of Garratt & Hemphrey of Nottingham.

1

4

2

3

1

1. The Scammell R8 'Routeman I' was only built from late 1959 to 1962 and this Gardner 6LX-engined example dates from the last year of production. Less than a hundred of these models had been built when the Michelotti-cabbed 'Routeman II' was launched in 1962. A Leyland power unit was optional.

2. An early example of the Routeman I in service with United Molasses, a large user of Scammell Rigid Eights for many years.

3. From the first year of production of the new Routeman II this 1962 example served with the Chapman Group in Bradford.

4. Making its debut at the 1968 Earls Court Show the revised Routeman II featured an Albion hub-reduction, double drive rear bogie, making it more suited to tipper application. This Denniff vehicle went into service some time after August 1969.

4

One manufacturer who briefly entered the rigid eight wheeler market was Seddon Diesel Vehicles Ltd of Oldham. Between 1958 and 1964 they offered two versions of their SD8/DD8 (single or double drive), this being the second type launched in 1962. Officially the designation at that time for this single drive model had become 24-8-6LX. The 6LX stood for the 150 bhp Gardner power unit. This well proportioned 14ft wheelbase bulk sugar tanker was, at the time of this photograph, based at BRS Wellington Depot in Shropshire.

1

2

1. A long wheelbase tipper based on the 1966 single drive Routeman II chassis, in operation with the well-known Oliver Hart company from Coppull, Lancs.

2. A 17ft 9in wheelbase 24-8-6LX trailing axle eight wheeled bulk oil tanker in the dark blue livery of GLS Transport from Whetstone in North London, parked up on a freezing winter's morning just off the Great North Road at Sandy.

3. An example of a DD8 in the fleet of Dutton's Blackburn Brewery, part of the Whitbread Group. The vehicle, which was originally based at their Chiswell Street Brewery in London, was powered by an AEC 6-cylinder diesel. It is mounted with an 80-barrel tank body.

4. A 1962 long wheelbase flat belonging to R Barker of Burscough near Ormskirk. This machine suffered the fate of many rigid eights of the period when it was cut down into a 'Chinese Six' three axle tractor unit in order to haul 12m containers as an artic.

5. Dating from the same year is 121DBU, one of a number of Seddon Diesel rigid eights from the well-known fleet of Athersmith Bros of Barrow-in-Furness.

3

4

5

A R T I

C S

In the early Sixties artics still took second place to the traditional rigid eight on long distance general haulage in the UK. The 1964 regulations reversed their roles. After the regulations took effect sales of heavy artics expanded rapidly. Many hauliers had existing rigids converted into fifth wheel tractors when they switched to artic operation.

The UK market attracted a number of European manufacturers and the late Sixties saw an influx of tractor units from manufacturers such as Volvo, Scania and Mercedes. Although leading British manufacturers had for many years supplied large heavy duty artics to such overseas markets as Australia and South Africa, the new breed of 32-ton high powered artic had to be tailored to the UK operator where low unladen weight and limited overall length were important considerations.

Ranking as one of the most adventurous cab designs of the decade, the Atkinson 'Viewline' sought to provide drivers with conditions befitting the long-haul motorway age. Underneath the boldly styled cab it was a standard 30-ton gcw 'Silver Knight' powered by a 180 bhp Gardner 6LXB. The first Viewlines had a stylish full width slatted grille but Atkinson users had a soft spot for the old fashioned 'outside rad' feature, which was consequently reinstated. It gave the vehicle a curious blend of the ultra modern and the traditional. The huge single piece windscreen gave an unrivalled view of the road ahead, the dash line being well below knee level. This bulk coal tipper was operated by Maidstone-based D A Johnson.

1. First real signs of the artic era came with outfits like this 1964 AEC Mk.V Mandator 24-ton gcw outfit with tandem axle TIR-tilt trailer. Note the old style brake hoses with palm couplings and the military style lashing on the tilt. Lep Transport Ltd were among the early British hauliers to engage in European work, mainly to France and Germany.

2. This medium duty artic of BRS is an AEC '5GM4RH' 18-ton gcw dating from 1961 and is powered by the AV470 engine.

3. An unusual machine to appear on British roads was the AEC 'Mogul' bonneted tractor unit. It was available with the '11.3' engine rated at 192 bhp and was primarily an export model. This 1965 example seen coupled to a lowloader was operated by Seymour Plant and is a left hand drive model.

4. If there is one articulated outfit that typifies the British haulage scene in the early Sixties it is this 24-ton gcw '8 wheel' combination consisting of a 2-axle tractor and twin oscillating axle 24ft semi trailer. The combined weight allowed on the trailer axles was 11 tons. This type was offered by numerous trailer builders under different names, such as the BTC 'Four in Line' shown here, the York 'Trans-Four', the Taskers 'Twinside', the Boden 'Twinline' and the Merriworth 'Osca'. This classic AEC Mk.V Mandator outfit is in the well-known livery of Federated Road Transport Services of Leicester.

1

4

1. By 1968 the 'Artic' had finally emerged into its fully fledged state virtually as we know it today. 12m semi trailers could be used within the 15m (49ft 2.5in) legal length limit. This well turned out 1966 AEC Mandator-hauled outfit is seen heading south on the A1 to London from its home base at Munro's Transport, Aberdeen.

2. In the mid Sixties one began to see the slightly incongruous combination of familiar tractor units, such as this AEC 'Ergo' from BRS, hitched to 'foreign' trailers. This distinctly German-looking tilt with wide spread 20 tonne bogie looks almost too big for a British unit.

3. Perhaps this 'AV691' (205 bhp) powered TG6R Mammoth Major unit on a wheelbase of 11ft 6in would be more 'at home' under the big tilt shown above. This 1966 machine, shod on super singles at the rear, is the double-drive 32-ton gcw unit representing AEC's biggest domestic model. It was in the service of Express Dairy on long distance bulk milk haulage.

4. If the double drive 'Mammoth Major' was too heavy at 7.3 tons, you could save 17 cwt (860kg) by choosing this highly impressive Chinese Six option dubbed the 'Mammoth Minor'. This one worked in the Barking fleet of I Leftley. In this form the payload capacity was about 20.5 tons.

5. Unladen weight on this truly 'mammoth'-looking Mammoth Major must have been in the region of 12.5 tons leaving approximately 19.5 for payload, It is a maximum capacity double drive 5-axle outfit. Some such outfits with bulk tipping bodies crept up as high as 14.5 tons unladen, allowing for a meagre legal payload of 17.5 tons.

1

2

3

4

1

2

3

4

5

1. A close look at the 'pan diff' rear axle casing and the just-visible transverse exhaust behind the front wheel identifies this as a cut-down Albion Caledonian eight wheeler. Albions did not offer a heavy tractor of this type. Though registered as an eight wheeler in 1959, this outfit has been included in this book because it is very much a product of the Sixties. It represents the hundreds of old 24-ton rigid eights that were converted into artics. This one is a particularly good example.

2. Atkinson's apparent determination to shake off its old fashioned image during the Sixties first manifested itself in the relatively rare 'tin front' model, sometimes described as the 'Bodyline' cab. This well proportioned outfit came from James K Allen Ltd of Newarthill, Scotland. It was in a smart grey and maroon livery and the message on the trailer read 'Direct Service to the South'.

3. This is the kind of artic that Britain was more familiar with. It is an 18-ton gcw Albion Chieftain with the LAD cab. Registered AHX532A it dates from 1963 and was part of Robert Deard's fleet based in Finchley, North London.

4. 1961 Albion Clydesdale at 20 tons gcw. This particular vehicle was a rare artic version of the MMB Bulk Farm Collection tankers which were being introduced in the Sixties. Note the twin oscillating axle rear bogie.

5. Leading hauliers W H Bowker Ltd of Blackburn showed forward thinking by changing over from rigids to artics long before most other companies. By the time this 1966 Gardner 6LX 150 bhp powered Mk.1 Atki was added to the fleet, they were already confirmed artic users. This scene is at their old Hollin Bridge Street premises which were recently vacated in a move to Preston.

1. A classic UK artic of the pre '64 era. This 1961 T746 is in the typically British livery of H Parkinson of Cleveleys near Blackpool. The registration suggests that it began life with the large Scottish haulier Russell of Bathgate.

2. A neat little 18-ton gcw Albion Chieftain loaded with some not so little sawn tree trunks presumably destined for the owner's plywood factory at Stratford in East London.

3. This late 1967 3-axle double drive Atkinson 'Silver Knight' features the rarer version of the Viewline cab with the somewhat unflattering 'styled' grille. It is in the fleet of Factory Plant Removals Ltd, the plant haulage specialist based at Handsworth in Birmingham.

4. Among the post war 'pioneers' of heavy artic operations was British Road Services, the nationalised road haulage wing of the British Transport Commission. Major plans to switch trunk operations on to artics were under way in the Fifties and 'standard' maximum capacity outfits were being developed at the BTC-owned Bristol Commercial Vehicle plant. This vehicle represents the latter day Bristol 24-ton gcw artic rendered obsolete by the '64 weight increases. BRS, under the new Transport Holding Company from 1964, decided to buy off-the-peg tractor units. This Gardner-engined HA6G photographed at Tufnell Park Branch in North London dates from 1962.

1

4

1. A T3266C Cummins-engined Silver Knight 3-axle Viewline tractor hauls this bulk liquid carbon dioxide tank trailer in the corporate livery of ICI. It dates from late 1968.

2. An even more unusual outfit than the Viewline above is this bonneted 5-axle Pickfords bulk powder tanker. A 'BT3266' it has single 'outer' wheels on the third axle and singles on the trailer bogie. It bears Pickfords' fleet number M3411.

3. After the British Leyland Motor Corporation was formed Austin and Morris trucks were re-badged 'BMC' prior to eventually being badged 'Leyland', even though true Leylands were regarded as high quality 'premium' vehicles while Austin/Morris were mass-produced types. The new 'Mastiff' artic was quite a move up the scale for BMC – at 26/28 tons gcw it had the 179 bhp Perkins V8 engine.

4. This old style outfit with twin oscillating axle dropside semi trailer belonged to Welch's Transport of Stapleford. The tractor is a 1963 Atkinson T746 and is seen delivering bottled welding gas to a large factory in Luton.

5. An Atkinson TRS3266XB Mk.II cabbed Silver Knight of Northern Ireland Trailers who handled ferry traffic between Preston, Lancs and Larne, Northern Ireland in the Sixties.

1

2

3

4

5

Like Bowkers, referred to on page 99, Sutton & Son of St Helens were moving over early to articulation. This 1964 'Mk.1' T746XA with 150 bhp Gardner 6LX was typical of their growing artic fleet. Suttons were also operating a European service at this time. This outfit is seen near London's Finsbury Square in 1965.

1

2

1. When Bedford first introduced their TJ bonneted truck range they included tractor units, carrying on the old traditional 'Bedford Scammell' type offering. With time demand for this class of artic diminished and the 'J4A' was withdrawn from the range in 1966. This 1965 registered example in operation with East Lancs Carriers was among the last to be sold.

2. Dating from 1962 this is a classic example of the lightweight Bedford-Scammell automatic-coupling artic which was popular with urban distribution fleets in the Fifties and early Sixties. The mechanical braking system on the trailer did not meet the more stringent standards set by Sixties legislation and the type lost its advantage when tractor/trailer air lines robbed it of its 'fully automatic' benefits. The sign on this trailer is reminiscent of wartime austerity. A choice of 300 cu.in. petrol or diesel engines powered these TKs for 8/10 ton payloads.

3. Contrasting with the Phillips Mills vehicle opposite, this 1964 Leyland '370' powered KGA13 with BTC 'Four-in-Line' dropside semi trailer is firmly in the realms of long distance haulage. Harris Road Services of Lostock Gralam, Cheshire ran it, hauling John Summers' steel from Shotton. Bedfords offered a 400-engined version too, the KHA14 which had the Eaton 2-speed axle and a gcw of 18.25 tons.

4. On another type of long distance operation, this 1961 TK car transporter features a larger than standard fuel tank. It carries four new Vauxhall '101' Victors and a solitary Bedford CALV van. The photograph dates from early 1965.

5. Finished in a bright yellow livery this 1960 Leyland-engined HA6LL Bristol artic was one of a number on contract to Steel Peech & Tozer, the large Sheffield steelmakers. Its original fleet number was 3D745.

1. Taking Bedford into the realms of true long distance heavies this 1967 KMA 22-ton gcw outfit with four-in-line type semi- trailer was powered by a 466 cu.in. diesel. Its overall character is enhanced by Radcliffe Paper Mills' superb livery, the non-standard Leyland fuel tank and a nicely sheeted load. Even the film of road grime adds to its 'proper lorry' image. KMAs grossed 24 tons when fitted with the optional Eaton 2-speed axle.

2. Less impressive but nonetheless a nice looking machine is this 1968 'baby' from the Ford 'D' Series range. It is a 'D300' on the ultra short 6ft 4in wheelbase and powered by the 4-cylinder Ford diesel. It grossed a mere 10 tons and was designed for operation with automatic-coupling semi trailers.

3. A make which never appeared in large numbers, at least not in the heavyweight artic class, was Dennis. Built at Guildford in Surrey, this 1968 'Maxim' sported a 170 bhp V8 'Polly' (a popular nickname for Perkins) under its engine cover and grossed at 30 tons.

4. A dry day had blessed this utterly spotless ERF 6.4GXB/York artic tipper on its maiden run on Thursday August 1st 1968, when this colour shot was taken at Dunstable. The outfit belonged to Willenhall-based Heads Transport Ltd.

5. Operating mainly for British Vita of Middleton, Manchester, Blue Dart Transport Ltd ran a mixed fleet of mainly AEC and Ford artics. This Ford D800 unit coupled to a Boden boxvan semi trailer bears the address of their Enfield depot. The use of adhesive decals was increasing in the Sixties but, as this trailer shows, they did not stand the test of time as well as proper signwriting.

1

2

3

4

2

3

1

1. A well balanced two-stroke powered Commer 24-ton gross artic in operation with the Portsmouth-based Brickwoods brewery. This CC15 model had the TS3 engine, at that time designated the '3D.215' (215 being the capacity in cu.in.) developing 135 bhp. Note the huge transverse exhaust, with double silencer, discharging to the kerb side.

2. This heavy duty Dodge D310 24-ton gcw artic bears the livery of British Ropes. The D310, Dodge's biggest tractor at the time, took the 143 bhp AEC 'AV470' engine.

3. An attractive 'Boalloy' cab disguises the true identity of this Dodge '3143' artic designed for 18-ton gcw. A choice of the Leyland '351' Comet diesel or the Perkins 6.354 was offered on these models. This one is seen with a Boden single axle flat semi trailer.

4. The Ford Thames Trader range included a medium weight tractor designed for a gcw of 15 tons and powered by their '6D' diesel. This automatic coupling outfit, photographed in very poor light at South Ruislip, was in the fleet of Express Dairy. Registered 523AUV it dates from 1960 and is loaded partly with flat packaging material.

1. The style of British artics in the early Sixties is perfectly reflected in this ERF 'KV' from John Russell of Grangemouth, with its flat 'four-in-line' style trailer carrying a demountable container. It dates from 1962.

2. Even by 1964, the year it all began to change, the appearance of British outfits had not altered very much as this brand new Gardner 6LX-powered 'LV' ERF shows. Its single axle 24ft dropside semi trailer is very much in the old style.

3. Within a few years 5-axle 32-ton artics were commonplace and such magnificent machines as this 6LXB-engined 'LV' Chinese Six tank outfit, BDJ257H, from Suttons of St Helens could be seen. This model of ERF's was in fact quite a rarity. Only a small number were built and at least five of them went to Suttons. Five-axle outfits died out from 1972 onwards when the minimum axle spread limit was reduced to make 4-axle 32-tonners more practical.

4. Returning once more to the 'vintage' era, this 1962 KV-cabbed 6.4GX artic has the Gardner 150 and a single axle flat. It was operated by well-known Scottish hauliers D M Smith of Wishaw, Lanarkshire.

5. Still only allowed to run at 24 tons gcw and therefore carrying slightly less than a rigid eight, this very early example of the LV-cabbed 6.4GX has a tandem axle flat with old fashioned 40x8 tyres. Note the vertical pushbutton cab door handles. Peter McCallum were based at Airdrie and hauled a lot of steel traffic.

1

2

3

4

1. Foden's 32-ton 'Twin-Load' artic was a departure from the normal UK design, having a load carrying 4-axle tractor and a custom-built single axle semi trailer. The combined body length was only 10.06m but the potential for 12m plus was there had the artic length limit been 15m from the start, instead of only 13m. Less than ten of these machines were built, all of which are believed to have been two-stroke powered using mainly the Mk.7 engine. The unusual tilt cab fitted to this one combines some features from both the S24 and S34 and is in fact an S30. Registered RUP504D it began life at Foden's before being sold to F&F Robinson of Stockton on Tees.

1

2. Yet another of the twin oscillating axle jobs which were hated by tyre fitters because of the difficulty of changing the inner rear wheels. This one is headed by a very smart 'S20' of Dee Valley Transport, Llangollen. Note the roof-mounted air-horns.

3. An unusual deviation from the norm was Foden's 'half-cab' tractor. Whilst saving a slight amount of weight, allowing better engine access and preventing the illegal carriage of passengers, it made the driver's environment rather cramped. Note the enormous outrigger for the nearside mirror. This was one of a number of half-cab Fodens operated by St Ives Sand and Gravel based in Huntingdonshire.

4. A rare Cummins-powered Foden 6AC6/32 5-axle bulker with 'banana' tank trailer by Freight Developments of Lancing. This 32-ton gcw outfit with super singles on four axles was one of three to be supplied to Blue Circle in 1968 and operated mainly out of their Houghton Regis works. The trailer bogie featured Foden axles.

2

3

'Poetry in motion' might aptly describe this magnificent Foden 'S36'-cabbed Chinese Six 5-axle artic as it heads down the A1 in North Yorkshire. It came from the well-known Horace Kendrick fleet based in Walsall and represents the finest British-built artics of the era.

1

2

1. Though this Guy Invincible tractor dates from 1960, this shot was taken in 1965 at the beginning of the new era of Continental style operations. It is coupled to a TIR tilt of Evan Cook International Road Ferry. Operators were Regan Bros (Haulage) Ltd of East London.

2. This Guy 'Big J6T' 5-axle outfit in the livery of Tarmac Roadstone Holdings Ltd must have weighed in the region of 14 tons, leaving a legal margin of approximately 18 tons for payload.

3. 'Old Warrior' of Bucklands Sand struggles gallantly up the steep incline out of this Surrey quarry. Its radiator top-up flap, which doubles as the Guy badge, hangs open.

4. 20-ton gcw Guy Warrior Mk.II from the Birmingham depot of British Road Services hauling an exceptionally long single axle flat semi trailer along Luton's Park Street in September 1964.

5. The Guy 'Big J4T' tractor could be ordered with a wide range of optional power units, mainly from Cummins and Gardner. This 1968 outfit loaded up with drainage pipes features the Gardner 6LXB '180'. It is in the livery of H Bolton & Son of Dalton near Huddersfield, Yorks.

3

4

5

1. This extraordinary 6-axle machine is of a rare breed, being a Leyland 'Steer'. The model was launched at the 1966 Earls Court Show and is, to all intents, a Beaver with a second steering axle. Powered by the 200 bhp O.680 Power Plus 11.1 litre diesel it had the same 5-speed SCG semi automatic gearbox as the 'two pedal' Beaver. The outer axle spread of this tractor was only 10ft (the Beaver wheelbase) and the fuel tank was transversely mounted behind the cab. Front tyres were 9.00x20 radials whereas the rear axle took 10.00x20s. It could legally operate at 32 tons gross with a tandem axle semi trailer but in this instance it is hitched to a triaxle bulk powder tanker. This is believed to be the first Steer built which, after exhibition at Earls Court, joined the Bulwark Transport fleet as Unit 917.

2. Once staunch Leyland eight wheeler users, Sealand District Transport, a subsidiary of steel manufacturers John Summers & Sons Ltd, added this brand new Guy 'Big J4T' to their fleet in 1967. It was one of their first 32-ton gcw outfits.

3. Harking back to the old era is this 1965 Leyland Comet outfit of Fred J Wright of Selby, Yorks. It was powered by the '400' 125 bhp engine and grossed at 20 tons.

4. The Leyland 'Super Beaver' bonneted artic was a very rare sight in Britain. The Derby registration of this example means that it was almost certainly new to Rollon Transport who were part of the old 'Speedway Group' which included Oliver Hart, R E Mason, Coal Deliveries, Fletchers of Ibstock and Mayfair Garage. They were mainly engaged on coal transport.

1

2

1

2

1. A fine example of the old 'maximum capacity' artic of the pre-1964 era is this Guy Invincible-hauled BRS Meat Haulage outfit dating from 1964.

2. Ultra short wheelbase tractors were typical of British artics even in the Sixties and this 1966 Ergomatic-cabbed 'Beaver' is on the 8ft wheelbase. It belonged to Road Services (Caledonian) Ltd, part of the large Tayforth Group in Scotland.

3. The longer Leyland Beaver model was on a 10ft wheelbase. This one, in the fleet of H B & H of Newton-le-Willows, with its tidily sheeted load, is an excellent example.

4. In 'pre-artic' Britain of the Fifties and early Sixties the only commonly seen articulated heavies were the bonneted Scammell 'Artic Eights' and 'Highwaymans'. The name Highwayman was coined in 1960 following Scammell's entry into the Leyland Group in 1955. Scammells had always marketed the vehicle as a complete 'Artic Eight' but under Leyland's influence it was eventually redesignated a 4x2 tractor unit becoming known as the Highwayman and available with a conventional fifth wheel coupling. This early Sixties Highwayman operated with Harris Haulage of Grays, Essex.

5. A forward control version of Scammell's long established 'Artic' was the 'Handyman' launched in 1960 to enable the use of longer trailers. This 1964 example is shown coupled to an early style Continental tilt trailer of MAT Transport of London and Barking.

3

4

5

1. A superb sight to any lorry enthusiast is this London scene depicting a 1964 Scammell Handyman and a 1962 T746 Atkinson artic of Monks International Transport Ltd from Uxbridge, Middlesex.

2. In 1965 Scammell introduced their Michelotti-cabbed replacement for the Handyman – the 'Handyman Mk.III'. This is an early example photographed in Liverpool and belonging to the large tanker fleet of James Hemphill from Glasgow.

3. Also launched in 1965 was the Scammell Trunker Mk.II – a rear-steer 3-axled unit for 32-ton operation. An engine choice of Leyland '680', Gardner 6LX or Rolls '205' was available. This 1968 tank outfit belonged to Hull-based Arrow Bulk Carriers.

4. Dating from 1962 this smart little 16-ton gcw artic is based on the Seddon '7-tonner' model. 1962 saw the introduction by Seddon of the Perkins 6.354 in this model which had previously taken the Leyland '350' engine. This outfit appears in the livery of Yorkshire Imperial Metals Ltd of Leeds.

1

2

3

4

1

2

4

5

1. Looking at first glance like the later 30/4, this 1964 Seddon is in fact one of the 'pre 1964 regs' 24/4 models on the 8ft wheelbase and hitched to a BTC 'Four-in-Line' which were built by the British Trailer Company at Trafford Park, Manchester. The operator is Canbirra Transport Services Ltd, Glasgow.

2. This Seddon Diesel 16:Four artic took its power from a Perkins V8.510 170 bhp 'V' Diesel. It was one of a number operated by British Railways' road haulage fleet and is shown here coupled to yet another BTC Four-in-Line semi trailer.

3. An ultra short wheelbase example of the Seddon Mk.15/10 which is seen in the livery of Whitbread group member Tennants Brewery of Sheffield. Power unit for this 1960 model was the Leyland '375'.

4. 1964 Seddon 24/4 coupled to a tandem axle flat employed on steel haulage by G N Ricketts & Co of Ewenny, Bridgend.

5. By the Sixties Thornycroft were concentrating entirely on the production of specialised heavy duty vehicles like this military 'Antar' Mk.III tank transporter. It was powered by a 16.2 litre, 333 bhp diesel and in civilian operation it would be suited to 150 gcw. In military use it was rated as a '30 tonne 6x4'.

PICTURE INDEX